DIAB

A lighter look at the serious subject of diabetes
By Theresa Garnero, APRN, BC-ADM, MSN, CDE

Many of the suggestions in this book presented by LadyBetes are based on *Clinical Practice Guidelines* from the American Diabetes Association. They do not represent the views or policies of the American Diabetes Association. This book is intended for humor and informational purposes, and should not take the place of direct medical care. Please consult a physician and diabetes educator for an individualized plan of successful diabetes management.

DIABETease may be purchased for business or promotional use or for special sales. For information, please contact BookSurge at customerservice@booksurge.com or 1-843-579-0000, ext. 00. Please mention that you are interested in co-branding for the best service. You may also order individual copies or an ebook version by visiting www.booksurge.com or calling BookSurge at 1-843-579-0000, ext. 00.

SUMMARY: A diabetes cartoon book that injects a little multi-cultural humor into the otherwise serious side of diabetes, while providing generalized facts and tips about the disease.

ISBN 1-59457-011-6 (paperback)
ISBN 1-59457-091-4 (hardcover)

Publisher: BookSurge, LLC
City & State: North Charleston, SC
Library of Congress Control Number: 2004106372

AUTHOR'S NOTE

DIABETease was inspired by people with diabetes, their families, my colleagues, friends, and family.

When people are first diagnosed, they are inclined to fear the worst. The misconceptions about diabetes are ubiquitous. As a Certified Diabetes Educator witnessing the triumphs and struggles of people with diabetes, I've observed the need for more positive and visually inviting information. I saw cartoons as a way to fill this void.

I am in gratitude to my parents and siblings for celebrating humor and imparting its virtues; without this background this book would not have been possible. I wish to extend a heartfelt thanks to everyone who has supported and guided me through the process and challenge of its creation. You know who you are!

Though there were numerous sources of inspiration and assistance with this endeavor, several people have been particularly helpful and deserve special mention: Rosie Castillo, Michelle Barth, Robin Beckman-Jones, Onnette McElroy, Mary Wurth, and last but not least, my talented artista mother Annie Garnero.

Putting the "art" in art and science is one goal of this book. Another goal is to give back to the diabetes community. Half of my profits will be donated equally to research for type 1 and type 2 diabetes.

Until a cure is found, we need ways to make life with diabetes a little easier. Cartooning as a science-based art form is one such way, and one I hope you find enjoyable.

Hi! My name is LadyBetes.
(As in rhymes with diabetes ...)
This book is about my journey with diabetes, and insights I gathered along the way. Whether you are already an expert or are new to diabetes, a little humor is a good thing. Cartoons are like recess, so take a break and join me. But remember, I may be an expert on living with diabetes, but I'm not a doctor. For individualized medical advice, consult the diabetes experts. In the meantime, may you laugh and learn. In the back of the book, you will find a list of definitions and resources.

The Synchronized Diabetes Swim Team

*Living with diabetes isn't easy.
It takes a lot of practice!*

When I was first diagnosed, I didn't believe it!

My fasting blood glucose levels were above 126, which means I have diabetes.

You either have diabetes, or don't.
You don't kind of have it! Whether genetics or
environmental triggers caused my diabetes,
I'm stuck with it.

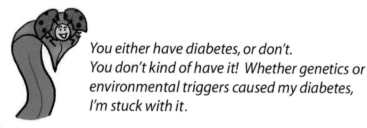

So I got educated and learned that diabetes can be controlled.

Controlling diabetes is a balancing act of healthy living.

Diabetes was first documented in ancient Egypt.
It has been around for a long time.

There are many types of diabetes,
including type 1, type 2, and gestational diabetes.

Some say the two main groups of diabetes are: in control or not. I say each person's diabetes is unique.

I started to exercise and take medication.

At first, it was a bit overwhelming!

Then I learned that I wasn't alone.
Diabetes is a worldwide problem.

*But I still don't understand why **I** got it!*

I don't eat a lot of sweets, but it turns out that doesn't cause diabetes.

"Talk about family history. Even our cat has diabetes."

And no one in my family's had it …
that we know of.

I finally had to accept my diabetes and make the best of it.

It took a lot of work to get my blood glucose levels under control.

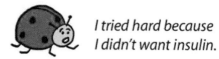

I tried hard because I didn't want insulin.

But I learned that insulin doesn't cause complications, high blood glucose levels do!

"What else can I add to your food diary?"

My family and friends helped a lot. They still do.

I started to count the carbohydrates or "carbs" in my food.
That's the fancy name for sugar or starch.

 One-third cup of rice has 15 grams of carb. That's OK. I can usually have 50 grams of carb for meals and 20 grams of carb for snacks.

I watch my portion sizes. I haven't met a carb I can't count. Do you count carbs? See a registered dietitian for a personalized plan.

I eat regularly and test my blood glucose often. It helps me control my diabetes.

Blood glucose testing keeps me safe, especially when I feel sick. It tells me if my glucose is too high (above 250), or too low (less than 70).

I want my blood glucose level less than 120 before meals.
Two hours after a meal, I want an average of less than 150.

My doctor and I closely watch my A1C. It is the gold standard for monitoring overall diabetes control. An ideal A1C is less than 7% and compares to an average blood glucose of 150 for the previous three months. Do you know your A1C?

I learned how a routine helps stabilize blood glucose levels. And that food, medications, exercise, and stress affect them.

 I try to stay active. It reduces stress and helps control my diabetes.

One thing is for sure. I eat better than I used to.

Eating healthily is important,
whether or not you have diabetes.

It took months to find the right
combination of what worked.
And for me, insulin was the key to success.

At first, insulin was scary!
My nurse helped me get started.
She is a certified diabetes educator.

My doctor and I worked together to find the right insulin dose. My glucose level came down, and I had more energy.

Insulin is not a cure, though. It helps me live well while researchers look for a cure.

41

Giving myself an insulin shot isn't that bad.

It's all the other things that make diabetes a challenge.

It's perfectly normal to get tired of diabetes. At times, I even feel depressed. That's when I reach out for support.

Sometimes my blood glucose monitor doesn't make any sense. So I call my diabetes care team to help me figure it out.

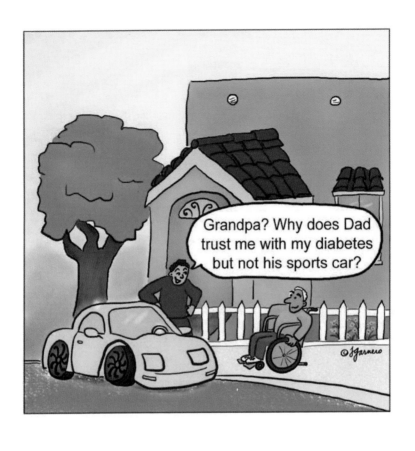

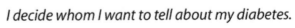

I decide whom I want to tell about my diabetes.

Eventually, I switched to an insulin pump. My blood glucose was all over the place, and the pump really helped with that.

My insulin pump has lots of options to keep my blood glucose in an ideal range. But not everyone needs insulin.

It even has a fast food conversion program. And a pastry correction factor. I just have to remember to pump, pump, pump it up!

I also try not to go too low. A blood glucose of less than 70 can be dangerous!

*Life is like diabetes. It's never perfect.
So I plan ahead for holidays and take
them in stride. Celebrations are to be enjoyed!*

I am expected to think like a pancreas ....
Do pancreases think?

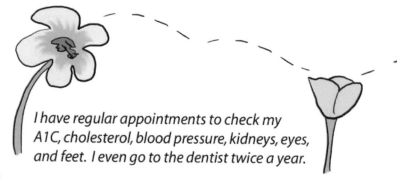

I have regular appointments to check my A1C, cholesterol, blood pressure, kidneys, eyes, and feet. I even go to the dentist twice a year.

I follow my dreams and have a lot of fun.

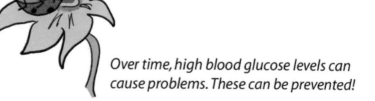

Over time, high blood glucose levels can cause problems. These can be prevented!

Life is precious. I enjoy it as much as possible.

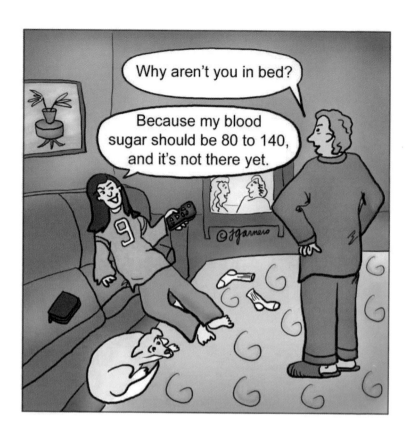

Well, I have to run. I'm going to check my blood glucose, then meet some friends at the movies. So goodbye for now. LadyBetes wishes you all the best!

Complications ARE preventable!

COUNT CARBS.

HAVE FUN!

E-x-e-r-c-i-s-e.

Check A1C every 3 months.

RELAX.

A blood glucose of less than 70 can be dangerous.

Diabetes is just a part of me.

Keep my feet clean and protected.

Insulin helps control my diabetes.

See the dentist regularly.

ENJOY FOOD!

When I think about all I've learned, it boggles my mind!

Take my medicine.

BE SILLY.

Check my eyes, cholesterol, blood pressure, and kidney function regularly.

CELEBRATE!

Reach out to my support team when I feel down.

Clean my room.

Call mom.

DEFINITIONS

A1C: a blood test that measures a 3-month blood glucose average, given in a percentage that shows overall diabetes control. (Also called HbA1C or hemoglobin A1C.) Experts recommend an A1C of less than 7%, which compares to a 150 blood glucose average.

Blood glucose monitor: a device that detects glucose levels within a small drop of blood placed on a test strip inside the monitor.

Blood sugar: layperson's term for blood glucose.

Carbohydrates: an energy-rich food nutrient. Found in all fruits, vegetables, grains, beans, milk, and yogurt, carbohydrates (also called carbs, starch, or sugar) break down easily into glucose for energy.

Cells: the smallest component of the body, visible only through a microscope.

Diabetes: a lifelong condition that interferes with the body's ability to get energy from food, resulting in high levels of blood glucose. For a diagnosis of diabetes, blood glucose values must be more than or equal to 126 fasting overnight, or above 200 any time of the day with symptoms, no matter what was eaten.

Diabetes care team: a group of medical professionals who help people live with diabetes. Examples include: primary care physician, endocrinologist, certified diabetes educator, registered nurse, registered dietitian, medical social worker, podiatrist, and ophthalmologist.

Diabetes symptoms: classic symptoms include profound thirst, hunger, increased urination, or unexplained weight loss; other common symptoms include fatigue, blurry vision, numbness or tingling in the feet.

Fasting blood glucose: a glucose level taken after at least 8 hours without food or other caloric intake.

Gestational diabetes: diabetes that develops or is first discovered in women during pregnancy.

Glucose: the medical term for sugar in the blood.

Insulin: a hormone made in the pancreas that allows glucose to enter cells, where it is used for energy.

Insulin pump: a small computer that releases insulin continuously to regulate blood glucose levels.

Insulin resistance: the body does not respond to or use insulin efficiently, which often results in high glucose levels.

Islets of Langerhans: clusters or groups of beta cells within the pancreas that make insulin. (Named after Paul Langerhans, who described them in 1869.)

Pancreas: the insulin-producing gland located behind the stomach.

Pre-diabetes: slightly elevated blood glucose levels (between 100-125 fasting, or 140-200 with food), which are not quite high enough for a diabetes diagnosis.

Sliding scale insulin: changing the insulin dose based on blood glucose values.

Type 1 diabetes: the body makes little or no insulin. (Formerly called juvenile-onset, Type I, or insulin-dependent diabetes.)

Type 2 diabetes: the body doesn't make enough insulin, or the insulin doesn't work like it should. (Formerly called adult-onset, Type II, or non-insulin-dependent diabetes.)

RESOURCES

American Association of Diabetes Educators
http://www.aadenet.org
(800) 338-3633

American Diabetes Association
http://www.diabetes.org
(800) 232-3472

American Dietetic Association
http://www.eatright.org
(800) 877-1600

Children with Diabetes
http://www.childrenwithdiabetes.com

Diabetes Exercise & Sports Association
http://www.diabetes-exercise.org
(800) 898-4322

International Diabetes Center
http://www.idcpublishing.com
(888) 637-2675

Joslin Diabetes Center
http://www.joslin.org
(612) 732-2400

Juvenile Diabetes Research Foundation International
http://www.jdrf.org
(800) 533-2873

National Diabetes Information Clearinghouse
http://diabetes.niddk.nih.gov
(800) 860-8747